Fritz Kreisler
1875 – 1962

Praeludium und Allegro
im Stile von Gaëtano Pugnani

für Violine und Klavier
for Violin and Piano

Fritz Kreisler
Klassische Manuskripte No. 5

BSS 29023
ISMN 979-0-001-10661-0

www.schott-music.com

Mainz · London · Berlin · Madrid · New York · Paris · Prague · Tokyo · Toronto
© 1910 SCHOTT MUSIC GmbH & Co. KG, Mainz (for all countries except USA, Canada and Mexiko) · © renewed 1938 · Printed in Germany

Praeludium und Allegro

G. Pugnani-Kreisler

Allegro molto moderato.

Violino

Praeludium und Allegro

G. Pugnani-Kreisler

© 1910 Schott Music GmbH & Co. KG, Mainz
for all countries except USA, Canada and Mexiko
© renewed 1938

Printed in Germany

BSS 29023

Allegro molto moderato.

Schott Music, Mainz 29 023

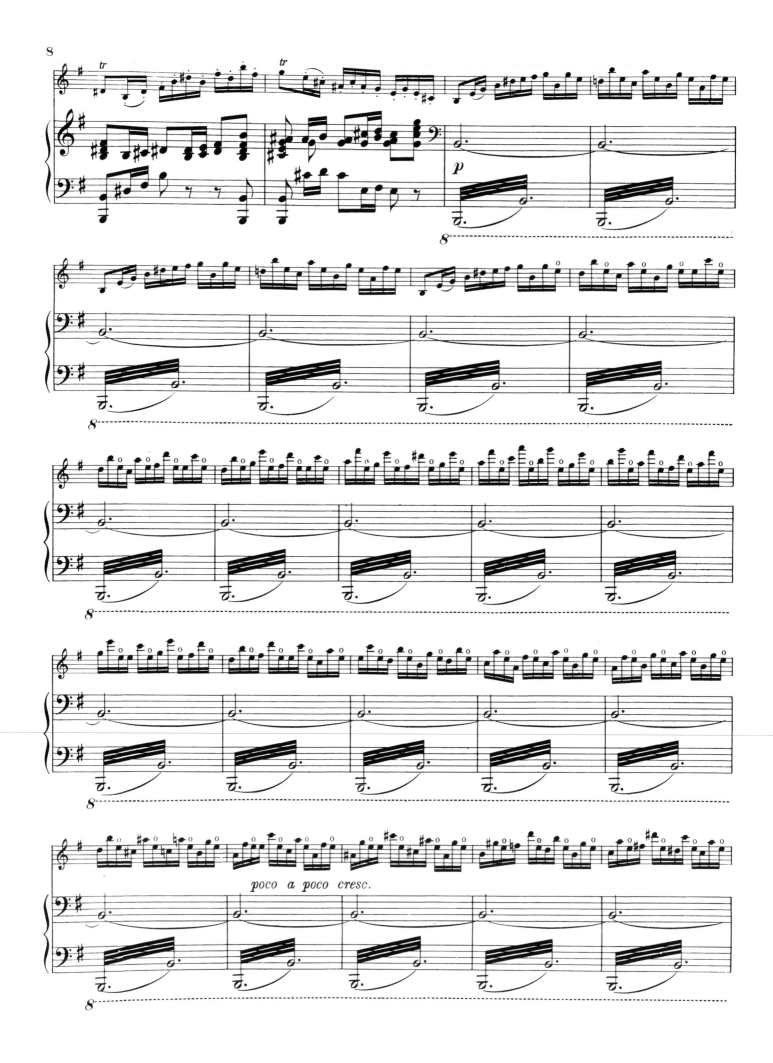